Many Little Beads

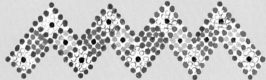

by Anne Sibley O'Brien
illustrated by Beatriz Vidal

Scott Foresman

Editorial Offices: Glenview, Illinois • New York, New York
Sales Offices: Reading, Massachusetts • Duluth, Georgia
Glenview, Illinois • Carrollton, Texas • Menlo Park, California

Robin has a bracelet.
It is made of many little beads.
White, yellow, blue, red, black!

It came from far away.
A girl got many little beads.
White, yellow, blue, red, black!

The girl made a bracelet.
She put on the little beads.

Many people looked at it.
They saw the many little beads.
White, yellow, blue, red, black!

A woman saw the bracelet.
She put it around her hand.
She looked at the little beads.

"I will buy this," she said.
"I like the many little beads.
White, yellow, blue, red, black!"

The lady got a box.
She put the bracelet in it.
She patted the many little beads.

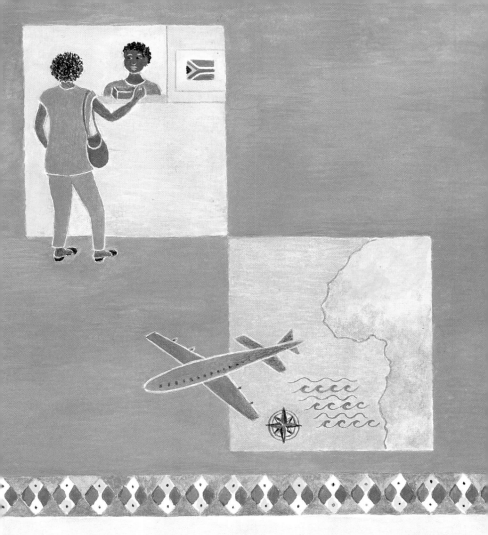

She sent the box back home.
It crossed the sea in a plane.
Inside were the many little beads.
White, yellow, blue, red, black!

The box came in the mail.
A note said, "Give this to Robin.
Give her the many little beads."

Robin's mother called her.
"My sister sent you a bracelet.
Come see the many little beads.
White, yellow, blue, red, black!"

Robin put on the bracelet.
She looked at the note.

It said, "A girl made this.
She put on the many little beads.
White, yellow, blue, red, black!"

Now Robin looks at her bracelet.
It makes her smile.

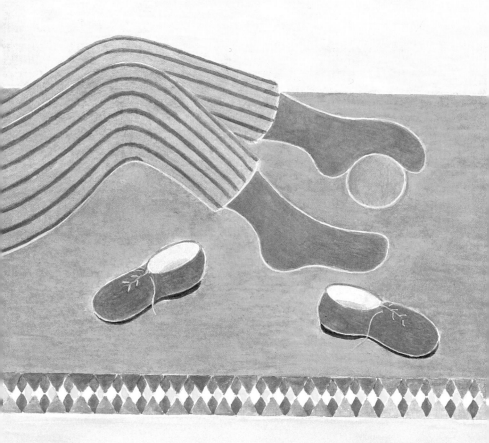

She thinks of the girl far away.
She looks at the many little beads.
White, yellow, blue, red, black!

Maybe she will go far away.
She will meet the girl.
She will have on the little beads.
White, yellow, blue, red, black!